Blue Crayon on the Cover
July 1, 03

LAKE MICHIGAN

A TRUE BOOK

by
Ann Armbruster

Children's Press®
A Division of Grolier Publishing
New York London Hong Kong Sydney
Danbury, Connecticut

Reading Consultant
Linda Cornwell
Learning Resource Consultant
Indiana Department of
Education

Subject Consultant
William D. Ellis
Editor of the quarterly journal
of the Great Lakes
Historical Society

The All-American lake

Library of Congress Cataloging-in-Publication Data

Armbruster, Ann.
    Lake Michigan / by Ann Armbruster.
        p.   cm. — (A true book)
    Includes index.
    Summary: Discusses the history, nautical stories, and industrial and
social significance of Lake Michigan.
    ISBN 0-516-20013-5 (lib. bdg.)   ISBN 0-516-26104-5 (pbk.)
    1. Michigan, Lake—Juvenile literature. [1. Michigan, Lake.] I. Title.
II. Series.
F553.A75 1996
977.4—dc20   96-2029
                                                                 CIP
                                                                  AC

Contents

Lake Michigan divides the state of Michigan.

The Third-Largest Lake

The United States and Canada are friendly neighbors in North America. Lake Erie, Lake Huron, Lake Ontario, and Lake Superior stretch across 1,800 miles (2,897 kilometers) of the boundary between the two countries. These lakes are called the Great Lakes.

CANADA

QUEBEC

St. Lawrence River

Quebec

GULF OF ST. LAWRENCE

Prince Edward Island

New Brunswick

Nova Scotia

Maine

New York

Vermont

New Hampshire

Massachusetts

Connecticut

Rhode Island

New Jersey

STATES

ATLANTIC OCEAN

Only Lake Michigan lies entirely in the United States. It is called the All-American lake.

Lake Michigan is the third-largest Great Lake. It divides the state of Michigan into two peninsulas. It also borders Wisconsin, Illinois, and Indiana.

The Chippewa Indians called the lake *Michi-guma*, which means "big water." Over time, *Michi-guma* became *Michigan*.

Early Settlers

The first people arrived in the Great Lakes region thousands of years ago. They probably came from northern Asia. Some came by boat. Others walked across the Bering Strait on a land bridge. Then they traveled down into what is now North America.

Wisconsin Indians gather wild rice.

These people, now called American Indians, were hunters and gatherers. They roamed the forests gathering berries, roots, and wild grain. They hunted beaver, elk, deer, and other animals.

The Old Copper Indians mined copper on Michigan's Upper Peninsula. Their tools were axes with antler-bone handles. They lived in homes made of sapling frames, covered with bark or skin.

This 1950s American Indian house is similar to the homes of past ancestors.

The homes were easy to build and easy to leave behind when the family moved on.

The Hopewell Indians lived in the valleys of the Mississippi, Ohio, and Illinois rivers. Then they moved into the Lake Michigan area.

The Hopewells, also called Mound Builders, were a very talented people. They sculpted pottery, polished stone, and made copper ornaments. They also made musical

This pot (top left), blade (top right), pipe (middle), and sculpture (bottom) are artifacts from the Hopewell Indians.

instruments. The Hopewells bound hollow tubes of bone together with bands of silver or copper to form flutes. They carved drums and rattles from turtle shells.

The remains of these American Indian cultures show that they knew how to survive in the wilderness. When the first Europeans arrived in North America in the 1400s, the Indians taught them how to survive.

Mound Builders

The Hopewells were called Mound Builders because of their burial customs. When someone died, they piled large amounts of earth on the grave. This formed a high, round-topped mound. Many such mounds have been found near the Grand River in Michigan.

Some mounds are in the shape of animals, such as this serpent.

The Fur Trade

In the 1500s, French explorers
traveled farther into North
America. Jacques Cartier
sailed the St. Lawrence River.
In 1608, Samuel de Champlain
built a trading post along the
river. It was called Quebec.
Jean Nicolet paddled a canoe
from the St. Lawrence River to

Early explorers of North America included Cartier (above) and Champlain (right).

Lake Michigan. He was looking for a water route to China.

By the 1600s, Europeans were looking for new sources of fur, because fur-bearing animals were scarce in Europe. Europeans prized fur coats and hats.

The French found the answer. Fur-bearing animals lived in the forests around the Great Lakes. There were many foxes, beaver, deer, elk, and rabbits there. And the American Indians were skilled in trapping. They also were willing to trade animal skins for trinkets and gunpowder.

The fur trade developed rapidly. The St. Lawrence River became a highway for the traders.

The fur trade lasted for nearly three hundred years.

The fur business brought great wealth to many Europeans. But it brought ruin to the Indians. Before the traders arrived, the Indians hunted only for their own needs. They used the meat for food, and made the animal skins into clothing.

After the traders arrived, hunting increased. Indians wanted the trinkets and gun-powder. Some tribes gave up all activities, except hunting.

After the traders came, the American Indians depended on guns for hunting.

Soon they became dependent on the Europeans for their survival.

A Melting Pot

Over many years, a variety of Northern Europeans settled on Lake Michigan's shores. The settlers cleared forests and grew crops. They built canals for ships to move throughout the Great Lakes. They brought many European customs with them.

Dutch costumes and tulips are important parts of the Holland Tulip Festival.

The citizens of Holland, Michigan, still celebrate their Dutch customs at the annual Holland Tulip Festival. The famous Veldhar Gardens exhibits more than two million tulip blossoms.

German roots are seen in Wisconsin. This state produces a great variety of bratwurst, or pork sausage. Wurst cook-offs are popular at the annual Oktoberfests.

People celebrate Oktoberfest with a colorful parade (above). A man cooks bratwurst over a blazing fire (right).

Door County in Wisconsin
also attracts many visitors. The
Scandinavian immigrants who
settled there created the "fish
boil." They cook whitefish,
fresh from Lake Michigan, with
potatoes and onions in a huge
steaming pot. Everyone enjoys
a fish boil!

25

Chicago

Chicago, Illinois, extends about 25 miles (40 km) along the south-west shore of Lake Michigan. The city is one of the busiest ports in the United States.

At Chicago, the Great Lakes connect with the Mississippi River system. And, after the opening of the St. Lawrence Seaway in 1959, Chicago

Chicago in the 1800s (above) and today (right)

became a seaport. The seaway connects the Great Lakes to the Atlantic Ocean. Today, the port of Chicago handles millions of tons of raw materials, produce, and manufactured goods.

The city is big in many ways. About three million people live in Chicago. It has one of the world's tallest buildings and the world's largest grain market. And if that's not enough, add the world's biggest post office building and the world's busiest airport to the list!

Chicago's lakefront extends along Lake Michigan. Millions of people come to enjoy its beautiful view.

The Sears Tower—once the world's tallest building (right), the old Chicago Post Office (below), and Chicago's beautiful lakefront (bottom)

Pollution

At one time, Chicago's waste was discharged into the Chicago River—also known as "the river that flows backward." Until 1900, the river flowed directly into Lake Michigan. Then engineers reversed the flow to prevent sewage from polluting the lake. Lake Michigan provides the city's water supply.

Waste from industries on Lake Michigan may cause pollution.

Many towns and industries developed on the southern part of Lake Michigan. As that area grew, untreated sewage flowed into the lake from Wisconsin cities. Industrial waste from Chicago and Gary, Indiana, added to the mess. Some beaches were closed to swimmers.

Polluted water can be dangerous to the animals and people around Lake Michigan.

In the 1960s, people tried to clean up the Great Lakes. Sewage plants were modernized. Environmental laws were enforced. Gradually, the condition of the lakes improved.

Dangerous Fish

Fisheries on the Great Lakes are a valuable resource. The fishing industry brings in millions of dollars yearly. The lake trout and whitefish found in Lake Michigan are prize catches. But these fish became prey to the sea lamprey.

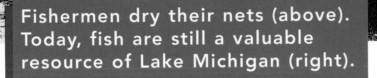

Fishermen dry their nets (above). Today, fish are still a valuable resource of Lake Michigan (right).

The lamprey resembles an eel. It has a circular set of short, sharp teeth in a suction mouth that can attach to another fish and kill it in one grasp.

By the late 1950s, lampreys had killed off many fish of the Great Lakes. The government took action. Barriers were used to keep lampreys out of the lakes. A chemical that kills lampreys, but does not harm other fish, was put into the water. By the mid-1960s, the number of lampreys in the Great Lakes rapidly decreased.

The lamprey's mouth is like a suction cup (right). Lampreys are long and snakelike (below).

A forest in northern Wisconsin (above), where loggers once transported heavy loads of logs (right)

Logging

Before settlers arrived, thickly wooded forests grew in the Great Lakes region. After the Revolutionary War (1775–1783), people began moving into this wilderness.

The white pine trees that grew in Michigan and Wisconsin had the best wood for general use. By 1900, one-third of these trees

When too many logs were transported on a river, log jams were common (left). Every logging operation had a mark to help identify its own logs (right).

were destroyed. The settlers cut down trees to build houses, churches, barns, and schools.

The men who chopped down trees were called loggers, or lumberjacks. Many stories soon developed about these men.

Tall Tales

After a tiring day cutting logs, lumberjacks would rest in the evenings. They would tell stories by the fire. One tale was about a giant lumberjack named Paul Bunyan. People claimed he was born in the woods of Michigan or Minnesota.

Paul Bunyan could stride over mountains. He could cut down a pine tree with one sweep of his ax. Some said that Paul scooped out the Great Lakes because he wanted drinking water for Babe, his giant blue ox!

Women celebrate their Dutch traditions.

Lake Michigan Today

The Lake Michigan region is home to many ethnic groups. Today, Germans, Dutch, and Scandinavians celebrate their customs, along with those of newer arrivals from around the globe. Tradition is a part of modern life.

People enjoy a beach on Lake Michigan.

Many natural wonders are still found there. Thickly wooded forests still cover northern Wisconsin and Michigan. The Sleeping Bear Sand Dunes still rise 465 feet (142 meters) above the lake.

Lake Michigan is truly a combination of the old and the new.

The Sleeping Bear Sand Dunes are a challenge for climbers.

To Find Out More

Here are more places where you can explore Lake Michigan and the states around it:

Books

Aylesworth, Thomas G. and Virginia L. **State Reports: Western Great Lakes.** Chelsea House Publishers, 1991.

Fradin, Dennis Brindell. **Michigan.** Children's Press, 1992.

Fradin, Dennis Brindell. **Wisconsin.** Children's Press, 1992.

Gleeson, Brian. **Paul Bunyan**. Picture Book Studios, 1991.

Pfeiffer, Christine. **Chicago**. Dillon Press, 1988.

Swain, Gwenyth. **Indiana.** Lerner Publications, 1992.

Organizations

Great Lakes Commission
400 Fourth St.
ARGUS II Bldg.
Ann Arbor, MI 48103-4816
(313) 665-9135
glc@glc.org

Michigan Travel Bureau
P.O. Box 30226
Lansing, MI 48909
1-800-5432-YES

Wisconsin Tourism Development

123 W. Washington Ave.
P.O. Box 7606
Madison, WI 53707
1-800-432-TRIP

Tour Lake Michigan

*http://www.great-lakes.
net:2200/places/watsheds/
michigan/michigan.html*

Take a tour of the Great
Lakes, uncover geographic
and scientific facts, and find
out about ecological pro-
grams concerned with Lake
Michigan.

Visit Chicago

*http://www.great-lakes.
net:2200/partners/GLC/pub
/circle/illinois.html*

Discover the countless
attractions of Lake
Michigan's shoreline and
Chicago's skyline.

Explore Wisconsin

*http://www.great-lakes.
net:2200/partners/GLC/pub
/circle/wisc.html*

Board a World War II sub-
marine, explore island
caves, and ride a steam
train. See all that Wisconsin
has to offer, including
Apostle Islands National
Lakeshore and the Green
Bay Packer's Hall of Fame.

Facts and figures about the Great Lakes

*http://www.great-lakes.
net:2200/refdesk/almanac/
almanac.html*

Includes information about
populations and the region.

Discover Indiana

*http://www.great-lakes.
net:2200/partners/GLC/pub
/circle/indiana.html*

This online site brings you
to Indiana's Lake Michigan
shores, where you'll find
lots to do!

Important Words

canal man-made waterway for boats

custom ways and traditions of a group of people

discharge pour into

ethnic relating to groups of people of a common race or tradition

immigrant person who travels to a new country to make a home

peninsula land surrounded by water on three sides

predator animal that kills other animals for food

sapling tree in its early growth stages

sewage water and waste carried by a drain

Index

Meet the Author

Living in Ohio, close to the Great Lakes, Ann Armbruster pursues her interest in history. A former English teacher and school librarian, she is the author of many books for children.